Kenya

Helen Arnold

RSVP

RAINTREE
STECK-VAUGHN
P U B L I S H E R S
The Steck-Vaughn Company

Austin, Texas

Published by Raintree Steck-Vaughn Publishers, an imprint of Steck-Vaughn Company

A ZOË BOOK

Editors: Kath Davies, Pam Wells
Design: Sterling Associates
Map: Julian Baker
Production: Grahame Griffiths

Library of Congress Cataloging-in-Publication Data

Arnold, Helen.
    Kenya / Helen Arnold.
        p. cm. — (Postcards from)
    "A Zoë Book"
    Includes index.
    Summary: A collection of fictional postcards, written as if by young people visiting Kenya, describes various sights and life in this African country.
    ISBN 0-8172-4024-1 (hardcover). — ISBN 0-8172-6207-5 (softcover)
    1. Kenya—Description and travel—Juvenile literature.
    [1. Kenya—Description and travel. 2. Postcards.] I. Title. II. Series.
DT433.527. A76 1997
916.76204'4—dc20   95–52928
                                                                    CIP
                                                                    AC

Printed and bound in the United States
1 2 3 4 5 6 7 8 9 0 WZ 99 98 97 96

Photographic acknowledgments

The publishers wish to acknowledge, with thanks, the following photographic sources:

Allsport / Clive Brunskill 28; Gina Corrigan 6; / Global Pictures 10; / Robert Harding Picture Library 26; The Hutchison Library / Tim Beddow 20; / John Hatt 22; Alan Becker / The Image Bank 14; Impact Photos / James Barlow - cover r ; / Piers Cavendish - cover tl; / Jorn Stjerneklar - cover bl; / Christophe Bluntzer - title page, 16; / Caroline Penn 18; / Yann Arthusbertrand 24; Frank Spooner Pictures 12; Zefa 6.

The publishers have made every effort to trace the copyright holders, but if they have inadvertently overlooked any, they will be pleased to make the necessary arrangement at the first opportunity.

Contents

All the words that appear in **bold** are explained in the Glossary on page 30.

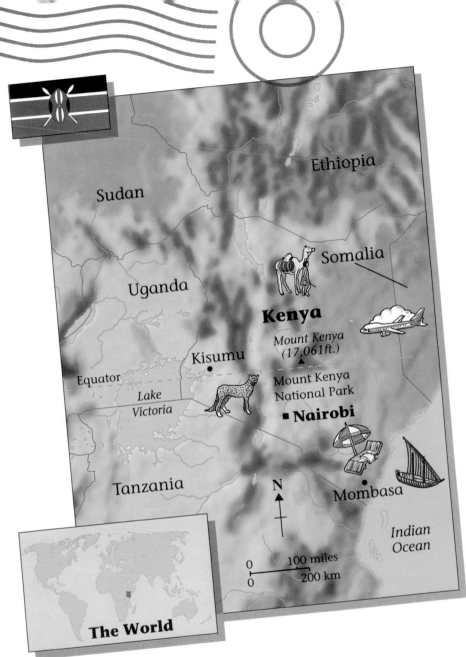

Ethiopia

Sudan

Somalia

Uganda

Kenya

Mount Kenya
(17,061ft.)

Kisumu

Mount Kenya
National Park

Equator

Lake
Victoria

■ **Nairobi**

Tanzania

N

Mombasa

Indian
Ocean

0   100 miles
0   200 km

The World

A big map of Kenya
and a small map of the world

Dear Mike,

We are in Africa. This country is called Kenya. It took more than 22 hours for the plane to fly here from Los Angeles. Kenya is marked in red on the small map. It lies across the **Equator**.

Your friend,

Greg

P.S. Dad says that Kenya is as big as France, but not as many people live in Kenya. Most Kenyans live in the south of their country.

A bird's-eye view of the city of Nairobi

Dear Penny,

We are staying in Nairobi. It is the **capital** city of Kenya. I like the stores here. They are full of baskets and wooden carvings. There are **tourists** everywhere.

Love,

Helen

P.S. Mom says that one and a half million people live in Nairobi. Many people speak a language called Swahili. In the city, most Kenyan people speak English, too.

A food market in Nairobi

Dear Sam,

We went to this market in Nairobi. People eat a special stew here called *Nyama Choma*. It is made with meat that is cooked on a grill. The meat might be goat or zebra.

Your sister,

Jean

P.S. Dad says he likes the food here. He paid for our meal with Kenyan money called shillings. You also need to drink a lot in this hot weather.

Cheetahs in the Masai Mara

Dear Stewart,

I am here on vacation with my mom and dad. A lot of tourists come to Masai Mara. It is a **game park**. The game are animals. We drive around and look at them.

Your friend,

Jerry

P.S. Dad has taken photos of buffalos, hippos, giraffes, elephants, and rhinos. They all live safely here in the game park. Dad says that we are on a safari vacation.

Outside the railroad station, Mombasa

Dear Julie,

The buses here are painted in bright colors. They are always full. People even hang on to the outside! We went on a train to visit the seashore near Mombasa.

Love,

Jenny

P.S. We were afraid to cross the road in Nairobi. There is **traffic** everywhere. There are big trucks carrying goods. People ride on bicycles, and there are hundreds of taxis.

Lake Victoria

Dear Winston,

We are staying at Kisumu.
It is on a big lake called Lake
Victoria. We cannot see the
other side of the lake. It looks
like the ocean, but the water is
not salty.

Yours,

Ken

P.S. Uncle Joe is taking us to a place where
birds called pelicans live. We have to wait
until the stormy weather is over. Joe says
there are storms here on 250 days of
the year.

Hikers with the peak of Mount Kenya in the distance

Dear Manuel,

It takes five days to walk, or **trek**, through the National Park to Mount Kenya. Some people called guides go with you. They bring food for the long journey.

Love,

Gita

P.S. Dad says that Mount Kenya is on the Equator. The weather is usually very hot at the Equator. It is cooler on Mount Kenya because the mountain is very high up.

Camels on the beach at Mombasa

Dear Gabrielle,

Today we went to a beach near Mombasa. We swam near a **coral reef**. We saw lots of brightly colored fish. There are more than 200 different kinds of fish in the ocean here.

Love,

Jacques

P.S. Mom says that long ago many Arab people came to live in this part of Kenya. Today these people still farm, fish, and trade goods.

The ocean and the old town of Mombasa

Dear Shirley,

Mombasa is on the ocean.
It is the second biggest city in
Kenya. There is a lot to see.
We went to the old town and
to see the boats in the **harbor**.
Then we went shopping.

Love,

Fern

P.S. Mom has bought lots of things. She has
got a *khanga*. That is not a kangaroo! It is a
dress that she wraps around her. It is cool
to wear.

Nomads with their camels in the desert

Dear Chris,

We have seen the mountains and the coast. Now we are in a hot, dry part of the country. It is called a **desert**. Not many people live in this part of Kenya.

Love,

Margie

P.S. Mom says that the people here are called nomads. They travel from place to place. They do not have houses. They live in tents. Nomads have lived here for hundreds of years.

Children join these runners who are training for a long-distance race.

Dear Dave,

Kenyan people love to play and watch all kinds of sports. Kenyan runners are world famous. People play soccer here, too.

Your friend,

George

P.S. Dad says that there is a big car race across the countryside every Easter. I wish I could go and watch.

Samburu boys dressed up to dance

Dear Luke,

People in Kenya love to sing and to dance. There is special music for every special event. I have a Kenyan friend. He has some good rock music tapes. He listens to Kenyan music, too.

Love,

Kate

P.S. We went to a big **festival**. It was called Madaraka Day. This is the day when the people began to rule their own country. It was on June 1, 1963.

A winning runner with the Kenyan flag

Dear Paula,

This is the flag of Kenya. It has three stripes on it. They are black, red, and green. In the middle there is a Masai warrior's shield with two crossed spears.

Love,

Suzy

P.S. Dad says that he can remember when Britain ruled Kenya. Now Kenya is a **republic**. The head of the government is called the president.

Glossary

Capital: The town or city where people who rule the country meet. The capital is not always the biggest city in the country.

Coral: Coral is the red, white, or pink remains of sea animals. Coral is as hard as rock, but it is alive.

Desert: A place that gets very little water or rain. Very few plants or animals can live there.

Equator: The line we draw on maps to show the middle of the earth

Festival: A time when people remember something special that has happened in the past. People often dance and sing during a festival.

Game park: A large park where the animals are kept safe

Harbor: A place where ships are safely tied to docks

P.S.: This stands for Post Script. A postscript is the part of a card or letter that is added at the end, after the person has signed it.

Reef: A line of rocks or coral close to the surface of the water

Republic: A country where the people choose their leaders. A republic does not have king or queen.

Tourist: A person who is on vacation away from home

Traffic: The cars, trucks, and bikes that carry people or goods on the roads

Trek: A long walk across country

Index